BULLETP
COOKBO   l. 2

Quick and Easy
Bulletproof Diet Recipes
to Lose Weight, Feel Energized, and
Gain Radiant Health and Optimal Focus

Madison Miller

Copyrights

Disclaimer and Terms of Use

ISBN: 978-1530583881

Printed in the United States

MAPLEWOOD
— PUBLISHING —

Contents

Introduction

If you are determined to live your best life, then you've come to the right place. The Bulletproof diet plan is a lifestyle designed to take you above and beyond what you thought was possible.

In order to optimize your life, you've got to optimize both your mind and body — and you can't do that if you're nourishing yourself with toxins. The Bulletproof plan helps you get those detrimental toxins out of your life (and your body) by providing a simple plan of foods you should eat, and those you should avoid.

You'll be glad to know that the foods that you can eat are foods that you love, that you enjoy, and CAN rely on as your energy source. The Bulletproof plan eliminates the fluff stuff that is filled with empty calories and chock full of toxins that destroy your inner map to success.

When you eat Bulletproof, you focus on whole foods like veggies and animal proteins — the stuff that's provided by nature. These clean foods have everything you need to function at the top of any game.

One of the things that is most difficult when you're figuring out how to incorporate a new way of eating into your life is easy meals. We've taken all of the guesswork out of your predicament so you can make beautiful, simple meals that fit your new Bulletproof lifestyle.

The Bulletproof Diet is the brainchild of biohacker Dave Asprey, who says he initially began his own research into diet in an attempt to tackle his weight problem. He says he has spent more than two decades researching how best to fuel the body to obtain optimal physical and mental performance. I will not detail the diet in this book as this is a cookbook, but I highly suggest you read Dave Asprey's Bulletproof Diet book to learn more. It is available on Amazon or in any bookstore in the health section. Dave Asprey's website is also a MUST stop on your Bulletproof journey. It has tons of information, and it is designed to give you tell you everything you need regarding every aspect of the Bulletproof Diet, including the scientific research behind the plan and the diet roadmap. To visit the website go to http//:www.bulletproofexec.com.

Going Bulletproof is going to have you feeling like a lean, mean, kicking-ass-taking-no-prisoners kind of machine. The Bulletproof Diet has taken the world by storm and for good reason, as it promises to increase mental performance and reduce weight. All this while allowing you to eat the delicious foods you love. It may sound hard to believe, but it works, and there are thousands of followers to prove it.

Going Bulletproof is going to have you feeling like a high energy machine. You will feel yourself getting lighter in body and stronger in mind. The key to going Bulletproof is forgetting about your old ideas about fat and protein. Going Bulletproof means embracing the fat and being careful to put the right amounts of protein from the right sources into your body.

This book has been designed to give the Bulletproof dieter meal options that respect the Bulletproof general guidelines. The meals have been created to ensure that you are getting the required amount of fat, protein, and carbohydrates with each dish. It is crucial that you get the right amount of nutrients so that your brain and body can function at optimal levels all the time.

Pastured eggs, and grass-fed beef and lamb are your best animal sources of protein and fat. It is these proteins that we've focused on. We've provided recipes for sous vide eggs, one of the best ways to cook eggs so you don't lose any of the benefits but still ensure your eggs are fully cooked. You will find delectable recipes for Aromatic Beef Tenderloin, (Offal) Lamb Stew, and Beefy Avocado Chili.

Good quality seafood is also a great source of heart-healthy fats, and you will find mouth-watering recipes including Wild Salmon Bake. There are also delicious recipes for low-protein days like Sweet Potato Bake, or Fennel and Avocado Salad.

Diet Breakdown

Each day will start off with Bulletproof coffee, followed by meals at lunch and dinner. If you are new to Bulletproof, then you want to do some intermittent fasting. That means lunch and dinner should be eaten within 6 hours of each other, and the lunch should be eaten approximately 16 hours after the previous night's dinner. However, if you've gone through the induction phase, then you can be a little more flexible about when you eat your meals.

Your meals are going to be composed of high fat and medium levels of protein. With your meals, you will have a small carbohydrate side dish that should be eaten shortly before your main meal, or shortly after. Just remember to eat this carb within the six-hour frame if you are in the beginning of your Bulletproof plan. Also remember that although you should have some carbs, those should be limited if you are trying to lose weight.

The meals included in this book provide you with the fat, protein, and carb balance you need to move smoothly along your

Bulletproof path. Lunch recipes are simple to make and portable. If you're at work when you need a meal, you can take the ingredients with you and throw it together in a snap.

For lunch, try out our special Salmon Cucumber Sushi Rolls or if you've got time, prepare a simple Beef Chili the night before and pack it for work. As long as you're not allergic, eggs are a great, simple choice to incorporate as a lunch option; we've got a lovely Fennel Egg dish that's going to do you good.

The options are endless for dinner because you don't have to be afraid of fat. We've created simple recipes including Bullet-friendly meats like lamb and goat so you can get used to including them in your lifestyle. Try out the simple Goat Curry for starters, and then move on to gorgeous Arugula and Currant Lamb Shanks.

We love SIDES! Sides make a dish complete and also provide that variety our inner spoiled child needs. You will want to dip into Ginger Smashed Sweet Potatoes and Broccoli Rabe on Sweet Potato Crostini. We are going to make you fall in love with your taste buds, and the kitchen.

You've made the right move getting on to a plan that is not only going to put your body into optimal mode, but also have your mind functioning at its peak.

The Bulletproof plan ensures that you are never hungry and your body functions like clockwork. This Bulletproof Recipes book is going to help you get from ho-hum to blow-your-mind amazing, and we're happy to be by your side.

Onwards and Upwards, Team!

Bulletproof Cheat Sheet

FATS
Grass-fed butter
Pastured eggs
Grass-fed animal fats (like lard)
Avocado
Coconut oil, virgin
Sunflower lecithin
Fish oil
Ghee

PROTEIN
Grass-fed meats
Low-mercury fish
Pastured eggs
Gelatin
Hydrologized collagen
Whey concentrate, clean

VEGETABLES
Note: Cruciferous vegetables should be cooked.
Organic when possible
Asparagus
Avocado
Bok Choy
Broccoli
Brussels sprouts
Cabbage
Cauliflower
Celery
Collard greens
Cucumber
Fennel
Kale
Lettuce

Olives
Spinach
Squash
Zucchini

GRAINS AND LEGUMES
Stay away from these!
EXCEPT white rice in minimal amounts

DAIRY
Dairy is not recommended except for grass-fed butter.

NUTS AND SEEDS
Coconut is recommended, other nuts are ok, but not peanuts

SPICES
Use fresh, whole spices, because store-bought mixes and blends can have toxins and molds.

Beef Recipes

Beef Tacos

Yes, it is possible to have tacos when you're Bulletproof, with a few minor adjustments, however. The important thing is that you're not losing the flavor and you're getting all the Bulletproof nutrition you need.

Serves: 4
Preparation time: 10 minutes
Cooking time: 4 minutes

Ingredients
1 ½ pounds pastured flank steak
1/3 cup walnuts
1 ½ cups cilantro, chopped
1 teaspoon dried oregano
1 teaspoon cumin seeds, ground
½ teaspoon paprika
Salt
1 lemon, juiced
Virgin coconut oil
8 leaves Bibb lettuce

Directions
1. Place the walnuts in a blender and pulse to crush. Add the lemon juice and ½ teaspoon of salt and mix. Set aside.
2. Combine the cilantro, oregano, cumin, paprika, and ½ teaspoon salt. Rub the spice mixture onto the steak and allow it to rest for 10 minutes.

3. Heat 3 tablespoons of virgin coconut oil in a skillet over medium-high heat. Add the steak and cook on each side for 2 minutes.
4. Remove steak to cutting board, and let it rest for 10 minutes. Slice thinly across the grain.
5. Divide the steak between the lettuce leaves, and sprinkle with the walnut "cheese". Top with cilantro, wrap it up, and enjoy.

Beef Chili

Chili makes for a super easy dinner or lunch, and all the way around you're getting a great balance of fat, protein, and carbohydrates for a clean energy boost. Although you're not going to be using your typical onion and garlic chili starter, the avocados give this chili a special layer of flavor that ensures you get a heightened avocado experience.

Serves: 4
Preparation time: 15 minutes
Cooking time: 35 minutes

Ingredients
1 ¼ pounds grass-fed ground beef
3 tablespoons grass-fed ghee
1 carrot, chopped
2 celery stalks, finely chopped
4 tomatoes, chopped
½ teaspoon cumin seeds, ground
1 teaspoon oregano
½ teaspoon cinnamon
1 teaspoon sea salt
3 cups bok choy, chopped
1 avocado, pitted and peeled

Directions
1. Heat 3 tablespoons grass-fed ghee in a soup pot over medium heat, add beef and brown.
2. Add the carrot, celery, tomatoes, cumin, oregano, cinnamon, and salt, and cook for 30 minutes.

3. Add the bok choy and avocado, and cook 10 more minutes, until the bok choy is wilted and the avocado is heated through.

Beef and Dill Brussels Sprouts Casserole

Casseroles are one of the easiest and most satisfying meals you can create. When you're moving to a new way of living, it's important that's easy for you to adopt. This casserole will help!

Serves: 4-6
Preparation time: 10 minutes
Cooking time: 30 minutes

Ingredients

1 pound grass-fed ground beef
1 ¼ pounds Brussels sprouts
1 leek, finely chopped
½ cup grass-fed butter, melted
¼ teaspoon cinnamon
Salt
Black pepper

Directions

1. Preheat the oven to 400°F, and prepare a casserole dish by coating it with a little melted butter.
2. Slice the Brussels sprouts in quarters, place them in the dish, and sprinkle with salt.
3. Place the leek on top, and drizzle with about half of the melted butter.
4. Add the beef on the very top. Sprinkle with salt, black pepper, and cinnamon, and drizzle with the remaining butter.
5. Cover the casserole dish and bake for 15 minutes, then remove the cover and bake for 20 more minutes.

Beef Tenderloin Salad

You will need to do literally 5 minutes of prep work the night before to make this delicious lunch salad a go. The beef tenderloin gives you a nice dose of protein and you get your gorgeous healthy fat from the avocado and virgin coconut oil.

Serves: 1
Preparation time: 10 minutes
Cooking time: 4 minutes

Ingredients
3 ounces tenderloin, thinly sliced
½ avocado, sliced
2 cups lettuce, chopped
¼ cup parsley leaves
1 orange, juiced
Himalayan pink sea salt
Virgin coconut oil

Directions
1. Heat 2 tablespoons of coconut oil in a skillet over medium. Add the tenderloin and cook for 2 minutes on each side.
2. Remove from the heat, and let it rest for 5 minutes. Slice thinly, cover, and refrigerate until ready to use.
3. Combine the orange juice with a tablespoon of coconut oil and a pinch of salt.
4. Toss the lettuce, parsley, avocado, and orange dressing with tenderloin, and enjoy.

Beef and Asparagus Sauté

Adding asparagus to your sauté will make you forget all about the traditional versions that contain a whole lot of onions — and ergo lots of toxins. This clean stir fry is a perfectly simple evening meal.

Serves: 4
Preparation time: 15 minutes
Cooking time: 10 minutes

Ingredients
1 pound beef tenderloin
1 pound asparagus, trimmed
1 avocado, pitted and peeled
2 tablespoons fresh dill
1 lemon, juiced
Salt
¼ cup virgin coconut oil

Directions
1. Slice the asparagus into 2-inch pieces. The beef should be ½-inch thick, slice it into ¼-inch thick strips and sprinkle with salt.
2. Heat 3 tablespoons of virgin coconut oil in a skillet, add the beef and sauté until brown. Remove to a plate and keep warm.
3. Place the asparagus in the same pan and sauté for 1 minute. Return the beef to pan and sprinkle with salt. Sauté for 3 minutes.

4. Place the avocado, lemon, dill, ½ teaspoon salt, and black pepper in blender and mix until smooth.
5. Spoon the beef and asparagus onto 4 plates, and serve with a dollop of avocado cream for some extra flavor and good-for-you fats.

Ginger Beef and Broccoli

This Asian-inspired dish has all of the flavor of take-out without any of the toxins. The ginger is an amazing antioxidant and flavor enhancer, while the beef gives you healthy fats and proteins. And as we know broccoli is everything!

Serves: 4
Preparation time: 10 minutes
Cooking time: 15 minutes

Ingredients
1 pound tenderloin
4 tablespoons grass-fed ghee
8 cups broccoli florets
2 tablespoons ginger, finely chopped
Salt

Directions
1. Slice the tenderloin into ¼-inch thick slices, sprinkle with a teaspoon of salt, and rub the salt into the beef.
2. Heat tablespoons 4 grass-fed ghee in a skillet over medium-high heat.
3. Add the beef, and sauté for 3 minutes. Remove to a dish.
4. Add the broccoli and ginger to same pan, and sauté for 2 minutes while ensuring that the ginger does not stick to the pan. Add a little water if necessary.
5. Return beef to the pan, mix the ingredients together, and serve.

Lamb Recipes

Sweet Spiced Lamb Shanks

These lamb shanks will take you to new destinations reminiscent of the Middle East. Some fantastic flavors come from the Middle Eastern region thanks to the generous and skillful use of spices. You'll get a nice dose of fat from the meat and ghee, while the grapefruit will give you much-beloved Vitamin C.

Serves: 4
Preparation time: 10 minutes
Cooking time: 1 ½ hours

Ingredients
4 lamb shanks
4 tablespoons grass-feed ghee
4 tomatoes, diced
½ teaspoon cinnamon
½ teaspoon cumin
½ teaspoon turmeric
½ teaspoon cardamom pods, ground
½ teaspoon coriander seeds, ground
1 teaspoon sea salt
2 grapefruits, juiced

Directions
1. Preheat the oven to 325ºF.
2. Heat the ghee in a cast iron skillet over medium.
3. Add the lamb shanks, and sear each side for 4 minutes.
4. In a bowl, mix the spices, salt, tomato, and grapefruit juice. Pour the sauce over the meat in the skillet.

5. Place the skillet into oven and cook for 1 ½ hours.

Lamb Shish

Although traditionally, many of us view lamb as one of those meats eaten during a holiday or a special restaurant meal, it shouldn't be. In places where omegas aren't so easily gotten from seafood, lamb is at the top of the list for obtaining those essential fatty acids in your diet.

Serves: 4-6
Preparation time: 5 minutes
Cooking time: 10 minutes

Ingredients
1 ½ pounds ground lamb
½ teaspoon cinnamon
½ teaspoon cloves
½ teaspoon cumin
½ teaspoon Himalayan pink sea salt

Directions
1. Preheat a grill.
2. Combine the lamb, cinnamon, cloves, cumin, and salt in a bowl, using your hands, until well combined.
3. Divide the mixture into four balls.
4. Shape the meat on metal skewers.
5. Grill for 8 minutes.

Spiced Lamb Meatballs

Who says meatballs need to be made from pork and beef? These lamb meatballs are beautifully exotic and full of fatty nutrients and flavor.

Serves: 4-6
Preparation time: 15 minutes
Cooking time: 40 minutes

Ingredients
1 ½ pounds ground lamb
½ fennel bulb, grated
1 tablespoon coconut flour
1 egg
½ teaspoon coriander seeds, ground
½ teaspoon cumin seeds, ground
½ teaspoon Himalayan pink sea salt
Virgin coconut oil

Directions
1. Preheat oven to 325ºF, and line two baking trays with parchment.
2. Squeeze the liquid out of the fennel, and combine it in a bowl with the lamb, coconut flour, egg, coriander, cumin, salt, and 2 tablespoons of coconut oil. Mix well.
3. Shape the mixture into 1 ½-inch meatballs.
4. Bake for 40 minutes, or until they are cooked through.

Fish and Seafood Recipes

Smoked Salmon Sushi

Wild salmon provides everything you want when going Bulletproof. This fish has got all the fat your mind needs to be primed for the second half of the day. This whimsical salmon sushi won't bog you down like the rice version, and in turn will leave you feeling light and refreshed.

Serves: 1
Preparation time: 5 minutes
Cooking time: 0 minutes

Ingredients
5 ounces smoked salmon, thinly sliced
1 large cucumber
½ avocado, pitted and peeled
Himalayan pink sea salt

Directions
1. Sprinkle the avocado with salt, and smash it into a paste.
2. Slice the cucumber vertically into long, pliable strips.
3. Spread the cucumber slices with the avocado mixture.
4. Place a slice of salmon on one end of cucumber, sprinkle with salt if desired, and roll up.

Chilled Smoked Salmon Zoodles

This meal has gourmet coffee bar lunch written all over it, and yet it's something you can whip up easily and quickly. You can prep the noodles the night before, or even in the morning. The few simple ingredients come together for awesome flavor and awesomeness for your body.

Serves: 1
Preparation time: 10 minutes
Cooking time: 2 minutes

Ingredients
5 ounces smoked salmon, thinly sliced
1 zucchini, spiralized
¼ cup coconut cream
1 lemon, juiced
Sea salt, to taste
Virgin coconut oil

Directions
1. Blanche zucchini noodles.
2. Combine noodles with smoked salmon, lemon juice, and coconut cream. Toss and enjoy.

Anchovy and Artichoke Salad

Many people have a strange aversion to anchovies, and yet they love Caesar salads. What do those two things have to do with each other, you ask? Well anchovies are that something…something that give the Caesar dressing that special flavor. Anchovies are full of healthy fats, so toss this up and call it a deconstructed Caesar.

Serves: 1
Preparation time: 10 minutes
Cooking time: 0 minutes

Ingredients
½ cup sardines, chopped
½ cup artichoke hearts, steamed and chopped
½ cup pomegranate arils
2 cups lettuce
1 lemon, juiced
Sea salt to taste
2 tablespoons virgin coconut oil

Directions
1. Combine the sardines and artichokes.
2. In a bowl, mix the pomegranate arils, lemon juice, ½ teaspoon of sea salt and coconut oil.
3. Toss all the ingredients together.

Crab Wraps

Real crab meat is very light but nutrient heavy; here we've paired it with the happy fat in coconut milk for a creamy result that will leave you smacking lips and sprinting through the afternoon.

Serves: 4-6
Preparation time: 10 minutes
Cooking time: 5 minutes

Ingredients
3 cups real crab meat, cooked
½ cup cilantro leaves
¼ cup cashews, crushed
1 teaspoon salt
½ cup coconut milk
8 leaves Bibb lettuce

Directions
1. Combine the crab, cilantro, cashews, coconut milk, and salt in a bowl, and mix.
2. Divide crab mixture among leaves, roll up, and enjoy.

Shrimp and Parsley Stir-fry

Parsley deserves a lot more attention than just as a garnish. This leafy green is full of vitamins and minerals and adds a ton of flavor to this simple shrimp dish. The coconut milk will give you a healthy serving of fat alongside the ghee.

Serves: 4
Preparation time: 5 minutes
Cooking time: 10 minutes

Ingredients
1 pound shrimp, shelled and deveined.
2 cups fresh parsley, chopped
2 lemons, juiced
1 cup coconut milk
1 teaspoon salt
4 tablespoons grass-fed ghee

Directions
1. Heat the ghee in a skillet over medium heat.
2. Add the shrimp, and sauté for 30 seconds.
3. Add the parsley, lemon juice, coconut milk, and salt. Mix and simmer on low for 10 minutes, or until the shrimp is cooked.

Wild Salmon Bake

Salmon is the steak of the fish world. This fish satiates while providing that hardiness that is lacking from lighter fish, thanks to its high heart-friendly fat content. Oh…and it's super simple to whip up when you come home in the evening.

Serves: 4-6
Preparation time: 5 minutes
Cooking time: 30 minutes

Ingredients
4 x 5-ounce salmon fillets
3 tablespoons grass-fed ghee
8 zucchinis, spiralized
2 carrots, spiralized
2 lemons, juiced
3 tablespoons dill
½ teaspoon salt

Directions
1. Preheat oven to 325ºF.
2. Coat a casserole dish with 1 tablespoon of melted ghee.
3. Place the carrot and zucchini the in bottom of the casserole dish, and sprinkle them with ½ teaspoon salt.
4. Top with salmon fillets.
5. Melt 2 tablespoons of grass-fed ghee in saucepan over low heat, and stir in the dill and lemon juice.
6. Drizzle the dill ghee over salmon and veggies.
7. Bake in the oven for 25 minutes.

Pork and Goat Recipes

Mustard Blueberry Pork

Blueberries provide a wealth of nutrients and anti-oxidants, and they don't need to be limited to your smoothies and desserts. Fatty pork combines beautifully with the sweet flavors of the berry and makes for a satisfying meal.

Serves: 4-6
Preparation time: 5 minutes
Cooking time: 40 minutes

Ingredients
4 bone-in grass-fed pork chops
½ cup organic mustard
3 cups blueberries
4 tablespoons grass-fed ghee
1 teaspoon salt

Directions
1. Preheat the oven to 325°F.
2. Sprinkle the pork chops with salt.
3. Heat the ghee in a cast iron skillet over medium, and sear the pork chops on each side.
4. Cover the chops with mustard, and add the blueberries to the skillet.
5. Cover, and bake in the oven for 35 minutes, turning halfway through.

Pork and Sweet Potato Lasagna

This is for those days you've saved up your carbs and are ready to let loose at dinner time. Although sweet potatoes are far healthier than their white cousins, they are heavy on the carbs, so enjoy with caution. This dish, however, is supremely amazing on a cold evening when your body wants to suck back as many nutrients as it can get.

Serves: 4-6
Preparation time: 15 minutes
Cooking time: 40 minutes

Ingredients
1 pound ground pork
3 sweet potatoes
1 cup coconut milk
½ cup water
¾ teaspoon rosemary
2 teaspoons Himalayan pink sea salt
Virgin coconut oil

Directions
1. Preheat the oven to 325ºF.
2. Coat a casserole dish with coconut oil.
3. Wash the sweet potatoes and slice into ¼-inch slices.
4. Place half the sweet potatoes on the bottom of the dish, and drizzle with a little oil.
5. Sprinkle the ground pork next, with the rosemary and half of the salt.
6. Top with remaining sweet potatoes and salt.
7. Pour coconut milk and water over the top, and cover.
8. Bake in the preheated oven for 40 minutes.

Sweet and Sour Pork Tenderloin

As long as you're consuming grass-fed pork you're in for a treat. Pork has all of the fat and protein you need on the Bulletproof Diet, along with tons of flavor. Here we give you a new take on your sweet and sour pork a la Bulletproof style – the best way, of course!

Serves: 4-6
Preparation time: 10 minutes
Cooking time: 50 minutes

Ingredients
1 ½ pounds pork tenderloin
2 nectarines, pitted and sliced
2 lemons, juiced
1 teaspoon Himalayan pink sea salt
4 tablespoons grass-fed ghee, melted

Directions
1. Preheat the oven to 325°F.
2. Coat a casserole dish with ghee.
3. Place the nectarine slices in the bottom of a dish, and drizzle with half the lemon juice.
4. Combine the salt, 4 tablespoons melted ghee and the remaining lemon juice.
5. Massage the tenderloin with the lemon mixture.
6. Place the tenderloin on top of the nectarines, and place in the oven for 20 minutes.
7. Flip the tenderloin, cover the dish and place it back in the oven for another 30 minutes.

Goat Curry

Although goat hasn't gained wide acceptance in North America as a standard animal fat and protein meal choice, it's gaining new acceptance through the Bulletproof community. The meat is hearty and succulent when cooked well and a curry is one of the best ways to start your love affair with this meat.

Serves: 4-6
Preparation time: 15 minutes
Cooking time: 45 minutes

Ingredients

2 pounds goat meat, in cubes
2 tablespoons grass-fed ghee
4 tomatoes, chopped
2 tablespoons ginger, grated
4 cloves, ground
2 cardamom pods, ground
½ teaspoon turmeric powder
½ teaspoon cumin seeds, ground
Sea salt

Directions

1. Cut the meat in 1 ½-inch cubes, and sprinkle with salt.
2. Heat the ghee in a cast iron skillet over medium heat, and brown the meat.
3. Add the tomatoes, ginger, cloves, cardamom, turmeric, cumin, and 1 teaspoon of salt.
4. Simmer on low for 45 minutes.

Goat in an Arugula and Currant Sauce

Arugula is a lovely green choice to add to dishes for its spicy bite. We pair the bite of arugula with the sweetness of currants for a delicious Bulletproof dish that's got your fat, protein, and carbs all in one bite.

Serves: 4-6
Preparation time: 15 minutes
Cooking time: 45 minutes

Ingredients
3 pounds goat meat, cubed
2 cups arugula, chopped
½ cup currants, chopped
4 tablespoons grass-fed ghee
½ teaspoon turmeric
½ teaspoon cinnamon
½ teaspoon coriander
4 cups tomato puree
Sea salt

Directions
1. Rub the goat meat with sea salt.
2. Heat the ghee in a skillet, and brown the meat.
3. Add the arugula, currants, turmeric, cinnamon, and coriander, and mix.
4. Stir in the tomato puree, cover the skillet, and simmer on low for 45 minutes.

Eggs and Poultry Recipes

Turkey Marinara

Although turkey for the most part is viewed as either Thanksgiving fodder or a super protein booster, this meat can be used to complement any on-point Bulletproof meal.

Serves: 4
Preparation time: 5 minutes
Cooking time: 30 minutes

Ingredients
4 4-ounce grass-fed turkey breasts
4 large tomatoes, chopped
1 cup tomato puree
¼ cup basil leaves, finely chopped
½ teaspoon oregano, ground
Sea salt
Virgin coconut oil

Directions
1. Preheat oven to 325ºF, and brush a casserole dish with coconut oil.
2. Spread the tomato puree in the bottom of the dish.
3. Sprinkle the turkey breasts with salt and oregano, and place in the casserole dish.
4. Combine the chopped tomato and basil in a bowl with 4 tablespoons coconut oil, and spoon this mixture on top of each turkey breast.
5. Cover the dish and bake for 30 minutes.

6. Drizzle each breast with a little coconut oil, and a sprinkle of salt before serving.

Turkey Avocado Sandwich

Pairing your super-powered protein with avocado makes this a perfect lunch to bulletproof you through the afternoon. All the ingredients are clean, keeping your body toxin-free and mind clear.

Serves: 2
Preparation time: 10 minutes
Cooking time: 0 minutes

Ingredients
4 1-ounce slices grass-fed turkey breast, cooked
1 avocado, pitted, peeled and sliced
1 tomato, sliced
½ cup cilantro leaves
4 leaves Bibb lettuce
Salt to taste

Directions
1. Lay a lettuce leaf on a flat surface.
2. Top with a slice of turkey breast, a slice of avocado, and some tomato and cilantro. Sprinkle with salt, roll up, and repeat the steps with the remaining leaves.

Buttery Bok Choy Omelet

You may be surprised to learn that bok choy is a member of the cruciferous family, and so it shares some of the benefits that you would get from broccoli and spinach. The veggie is a great source of protein and antioxidants.

Serves: 2
Preparation time: 5 minutes
Cooking time: 5 minutes

Ingredients
4 pastured eggs
3 cups bok choy, chopped
4 tablespoons grass-fed ghee
½ teaspoon salt

Directions
1. In a bowl, whisk the eggs. Add the bok choy and salt, and mix.
2. Heat the ghee in a skillet over medium heat.
3. Add the egg mixture and cook for about a minute and a half, then flip and cook on the other side for 30 seconds.
4. Remove from the heat and serve.

Fennel Egg Salad Wraps

As long as you're not allergic to eggs, they make a perfect Bulletproof lunch. They're quick and easy to prepare, and you can easily take them to go. Most importantly, they have a nice fat and protein combo that will keep you full and bulletproof.

Serves: 2
Preparation time: 10 minutes
Cooking time: 20 minutes

Ingredients
1 fennel bulb, trimmed
4 pastured eggs, soft-boiled
Sea salt
4 large lettuce leaves

Directions
1. Grate the fennel into a bowl.
2. Slice the soft-boiled egg and stir it into the fennel.
3. Add salt, oregano, and mix.
4. Scoop the salad into lettuce wrap, roll up, and enjoy.

Sides

Broccoli Rabe on Sweet Potato Crostini

This side is so good you're going to want it as a meal! The sweet potato deliciously replaces the traditional bready crostini and the broccoli rabe gives your body tons of vitamins and proteins.

Serves: 4-6
Preparation time: 15 minutes
Cooking time: 40 minutes

Ingredients
1 ¼-poundsbroccoli rabe
2 sweet potatoes
1 lemon, juiced
Himalayan pink sea salt
Olive oil

Directions
1. Preheat the oven to 320°F, and brush a baking sheet with olive oil.
2. Slice the sweet potatoes into ¼-inch slices and place them on the baking sheet.
3. Sprinkle the potatoes with salt and bake for 25-35 minutes, turning halfway through, until they are cooked and beginning to brown.
4. Blanch broccoli rabe, and mix with lemon juice, a splash of olive oil, and salt.
5. Spoon the broccoli rabe onto the sweet potato crostini and serve.

Ginger Smashed Sweet Potatoes

The thing about sweet potatoes is that they give you a home kind of comfort. This sweet potato smash gives you all that comfort plus the added vitamins and a mineral boost from its wealth of beta carotene.

Serves: 4-6
Preparation time: 5 minutes
Cooking time: 20 minutes

Ingredients
3 sweet potatoes, washed and unpeeled
2 tablespoons fresh ginger, grated
1 teaspoon Himalayan pink sea salt
3 tablespoons grass-fed ghee

Directions
1. Steam the sweet potatoes.
2. When they are soft, use a fork to smash them, and drizzle with the ghee.
3. Mix in the ginger and salt.

Sweet Potato Discs

These sweet potato discs will help you forget that thing you knew as French fries. These sweet potato bites give you the crisp on the outside and that softness you love on the inside.

Serves: 4-6
Preparation time: 10 minutes
Cooking time: 25 minutes

Ingredients
2 sweet potatoes, peeled
1 teaspoon rosemary
1 teaspoon Himalayan pink sea salt
¼ cup grass-fed ghee, melted

Directions
1. Preheat the oven to 325ºF, and brush the bottom of a baking tray with ghee.
2. Slice the sweet potatoes into ¼-inch thick discs, and place them in a single layer on the baking tray. Drizzle them with remaining ghee.
3. Combine the salt and rosemary, and sprinkle half over the sweet potatoes.
4. Bake in the oven for 25 minutes. Turn halfway through, and sprinkle with remaining salt mixture.

Creamy Coconut Spinach

Sweet coconut milk with spinach is the perfect side to a meaty dish. In the old days you might have had pasta, but this beats that hands down, thanks to its tongue-soothing creaminess and its nutrition high.

Serves: 4-6
Preparation time: 10 minutes
Cooking time: 20 minutes

Ingredients
1 pound spinach, washed and chopped
1 cup coconut milk
4 tablespoons grass-fed ghee
1 teaspoon salt

Directions
1. Heat the ghee in a skillet over medium.
2. Add the spinach and sauté until wilted.
3. Stir in the coconut milk and salt.
4. Simmer on low for 10 minutes, or until the moisture has dissipated and a creamy mixture remains.

Nutty Bok Choy

Sometimes the thing we need when we're on a new diet plan is variety, and this nutty bok choy provides that. The softness of the bok choy paired with a crunchy nut gives a whole new dimension to a traditional side.

Serves: 4-6
Preparation time: 10 minutes
Cooking time: 10 minutes

Ingredients
1 pound bok choy
½ cup cashews, chopped
4 tablespoons virgin coconut oil
1 teaspoon Himalayan pink sea salt

Directions
1. Heat the coconut oil over medium heat in a skillet.
2. Add the bok choy and sauté until wilted.
3. Add the cashews and Himalayan salt, mix, and cook for a minute more.

Zucchini Pasta

Zucchini is so very versatile and so very delicate in flavor that it makes the perfect pasta substitute. This dish is simple to make and pairs with most mains.

Serves: 4-6
Preparation time: 10 minutes
Cooking time: 10 minutes

Ingredients
4 zucchinis, spiralized
¼ cup parsley leaves
4 tablespoons virgin coconut oil
1 teaspoon oregano
1 teaspoon sea salt

Directions
1. Heat the coconut oil over medium in a skillet
2. Add the zucchini spirals and sauté for 3 minutes.
3. Add the sea salt, oregano, and parsley. Remove the skillet from the heat and mix.

Fennel Puree

Fennel is spicy and nutritious and will give you a fresh hearty mouthful of satisfaction. The added spice of fennel goes nicely with your fatty meats.

Serves: 4-6
Preparation time: 10 minutes
Cooking time: 0 minutes

Ingredients
2 fennel bulbs, peeled and grated
1 carrot, peeled and grated
1 cup parsley leaves
1 lemon, juiced
1 teaspoon Himalayan pink sea salt
3 tablespoons avocado oil

Directions
1. Combine the fennel, carrot, parsley, lemon juice, salt, and avocado oil in a bowl and mix.
2. Chill in the refrigerator for 30 minutes before serving.

Yam BAMS

The humble yam usually sits in a tiny corner of the grocery store, unassuming and yet full of gorgeous flavor. Yams make for a nice alternative to potato carbs and are just as satisfying.

Serves: 4-6
Preparation time: 10 minutes
Cooking time: 20 minutes

Ingredients
2 yams, halved
6 slices grass-fed bacon, cooked
½ cup parsley
1 teaspoon Himalayan pink sea salt
Grass-fed ghee

Directions
1. Preheat the oven to 325°F.
2. Coat a baking sheet with grass-fed ghee.
3. Steam the yams, and scoop out a tablespoon of the flesh from each half.
4. Chop up the cooked bacon and mix it with the yam flesh. Stir in the parsley and salt.
5. Scoop the mixture back into the yam, place on the baking sheet, and bake for 20 minutes.

Avocado-Cuddled Tomatoes

Yep, these guys are as cute as they sound. The fatty avocado really does cuddle the tomato to create a side that's going to blow your mind … or at least blow your main dish out of the water.

Serves: 4
Preparation time: 15 minutes
Cooking time: 25 minutes

Ingredients
1 avocado, pitted, peeled and diced
4 large tomatoes
4 pastured eggs
2 teaspoons dill
1 teaspoon sea salt
Virgin coconut oil

Directions
1. Preheat the oven to 325°F, and brush a casserole dish with coconut oil.
2. Slice the tops off the tomatoes, and scoop out the flesh while keeping the walls intact.
3. Place the tomato centers in a bowl, and combine them with the avocado, dill, and salt.
4. Crack an egg into each tomato cup, and top with the avocado mixture.
5. Bake in the oven for 25 minutes.

Cashew Rice

As we know, white rice isn't something you want to eat all of the time, but when you need that carb fix, it's a Bullet-approved choice. Here we add fatty cashews to balance out the carbs you're going to be consuming, and you get a nutty plus silky flavor.

Serves: 4-6
Preparation time: 5 minutes
Cooking time: 20 minutes

Ingredients
1 cup dry Basmati rice
½ cup cashews, chopped
½ teaspoon cumin
¼ teaspoon turmeric
1 teaspoon sea salt
2 tablespoons grass-fed ghee

Directions
1. Rinse the rice until the water runs clear, and drain.
2. Heat the ghee in a skillet over medium heat. Add the rice, cumin, turmeric, and sea salt, and sauté for a minute.
3. Cook rice according to directions.
4. Allow rice to cool for 10 minutes, add cashews and serve.

Beef Biryani

This biryani could be a main dish, if you weren't concerned with your carb count — but you ARE, so DON'T eat it all yourself! Beef Biryani is a local Indian dish infused with delicious exotic flavors. Pair it with a simple entrée that doesn't have strong flavors of its own.

Serves: 4-6
Preparation time: 10 minutes
Cooking time: 30 minutes

Ingredients
½ pound beef tenderloin
4 tablespoons grass-fed ghee
1 carrot, peeled and finely chopped
1 cup dry rice
½ teaspoon cumin
¼ teaspoon cinnamon
½ teaspoon cloves, ground
1 teaspoon sea salt
2 cups water or stock

Directions
1. Rinse the rice until the water runs clear. Cook according to package instructions.
2. Slice the tenderloin into ¼-inch pieces.
3. Heat the ghee in a skillet over medium. Add the beef, carrot, cumin, cinnamon, cloves, and salt. Sauté until fragrant, about 1 minute.
4. Add the rice, and sauté for another minute.

Zucchini Ratatouille

The traditional ratatouille includes a ton of garlic and onions; we've eliminated those here and made it into a nice simple side. The addition of squash provides you with added nutrients and the basil flavor takes it of the hook. Bullet awesomeness!

Serves: 4-6
Preparation time: 30 minutes
Cooking time: 20 minutes

Ingredients
4 zucchinis, sliced
1 summer squash, peeled and sliced
4 tomatoes, chopped
1 cup water
½ teaspoon thyme
½ teaspoon rosemary
¼ cup basil, chopped
½ teaspoon sea salt
4 tablespoons grass-fed ghee

Directions
1. Heat the ghee in a soup pot over medium. Add the zucchini and squash and sauté for 4 minutes.
2. Add the tomatoes, water, thyme, rosemary, basil, and salt. Cover, and simmer on low for 30 minutes.

Conclusion

We hope you're feeling fit and strong enough to take on your goals, your world, your everything! The Bulletproof plan is revolutionary in its approach, as it is as about perfecting your mind as well as your body. If you're someone that wants to perfect all areas of your life, then this is the plan that is going to do it for you.

The recipes included in this book are simple to create and should help you stick to the Bulletproof lifestyle. You're going to discover that cooking for your body and mind is a lot simpler than cooking for average food's sake. Once you've got a few of the staple Bulletproof ingredients on hand, like grass-fed ghee, virgin coconut oil, and clean whole spices, cooking these dishes is a snap, wink, and done.

Good luck on this amazing journey you're undertaking. In fact, forget about luck, you don't need it, because you've made a decision to Bulletproof and that's all you need. Get ready to take your life to a whole new level!

May the Bulletproof be with you!

More Books by Madison Miller

Printed in Great Britain
by Amazon

77127692R00034